GROWTH AND LIFE CYCLE OF LIVING THINGS:
FROM ANIMALS TO HUMANS

Life Cycle Books Grade 4 | Children's Science & Nature Books

First Edition, 2020

Published in the United States by Speedy Publishing LLC, 40 E Main Street, Newark, Delaware 19711 USA.

© 2020 Baby Professor Books, an imprint of Speedy Publishing LLC

Baby Professor Books are available at special discounts when purchased in bulk for industrial and sales-promotional use. For details contact our Special Sales Team at Speedy Publishing LLC, 40 E Main Street, Newark, Delaware 19711 USA. Telephone (888) 248-4521 Fax: (210) 519-4043.

10 9 8 7 6 * 5 4 3 2 1

Print Edition: 9781541959613
Digital Edition: 9781541962613

See the world in pictures. Build your knowledge in style.
www.speedypublishing.com

TABLE OF CONTENTS

As we grow up, we are called different things based upon how old we are. When we are born, we are called babies. As we get older, we are called toddlers, children, pre-teens, teenagers, and other monikers until we reach adulthood. All living creatures have stages of growth until they reach full maturity. How long this process takes or what is involved varies from species to species. This book will discuss life cycles of animals, plants, insects, and amphibians.

THE LIFE CYCLE OF ANIMALS

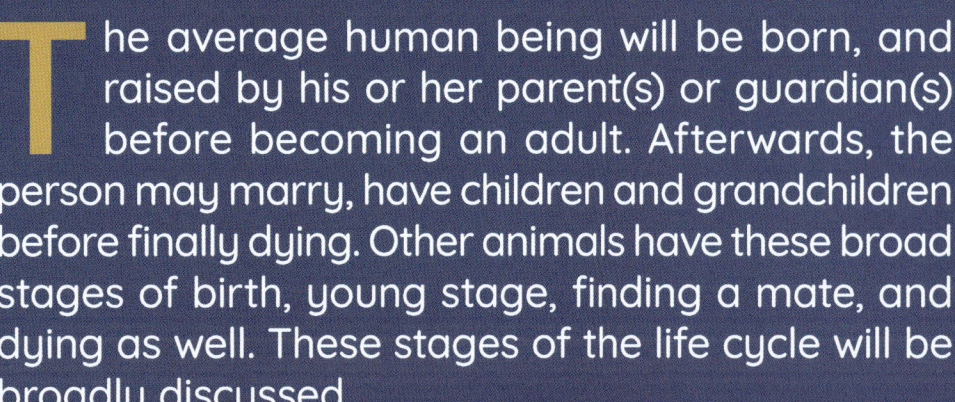The average human being will be born, and raised by his or her parent(s) or guardian(s) before becoming an adult. Afterwards, the person may marry, have children and grandchildren before finally dying. Other animals have these broad stages of birth, young stage, finding a mate, and dying as well. These stages of the life cycle will be broadly discussed.

Your parents will take care of you until you become an adult.

Birth and Youth:

Much of the animal world does begin life inside of an egg, rather than being born. The egg provides a barrier which protects the developing organism from the outside world. Examples of creatures that are born from eggs are snakes, birds, and fish.

Snakes, fish and birds start out as eggs.

Most animals are hatched from eggs instead of being born.

Most animals are hatched from eggs instead of being born, like humans are. Sometimes the young animal will be nurtured by both parents, while other times simply by one parent. In the latter case, it is typically the mother.

A caterpillar has to go through the process of metamorphosis before becoming an adult butterfly.

Once an animal is born, it enters a general stage which is called the young stage. Alternatively, it may be aptly called the childhood stage. It is at this stage of life that animals will have the most growth and development. In general, at this stage the young animal will look like a smaller, more vulnerable version of their adult counterparts. This contrasts with a growth period called metamorphosis. Metamorphosis takes place in insects and amphibians and through it, their appearances are radically altered.

A bird looking out for her young. These young birds are most vulnerable during this stage.

Two black crowned cranes performing a mating dance.

Reproduction:

Reproduction is a word that talks about how a species creates more members, in other words how they have offspring or children. Reproduction happens after members of the species have reached adulthood, or maturity. Some animal species will display bright colors or other special features to attract the attention of a potential female mate. Some animals may also have a special dance that they can do together. Depending on the species, some couples may choose to stay together or go their separate ways. Monogamy is a word that can mean having only one mate at a time.

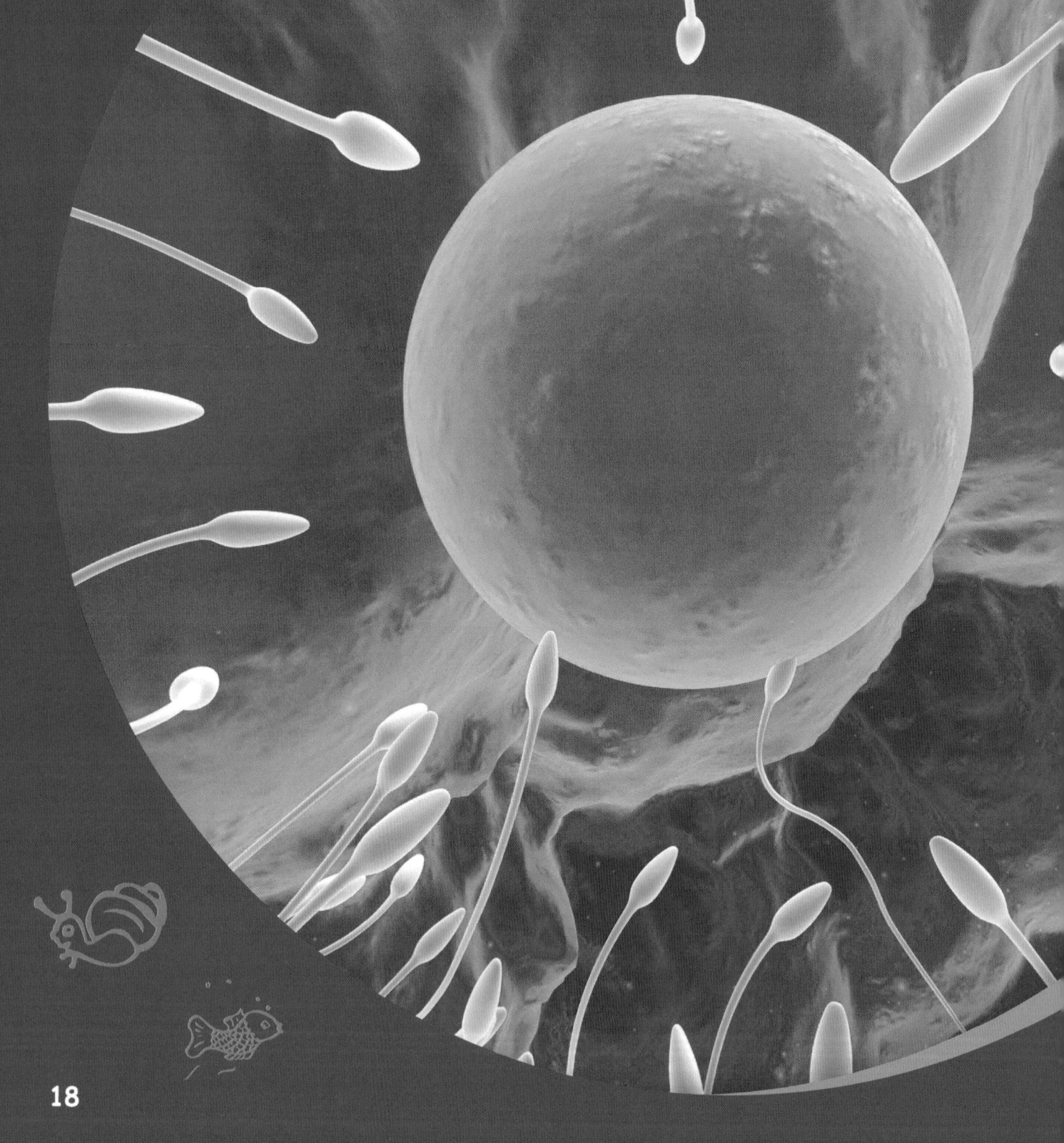

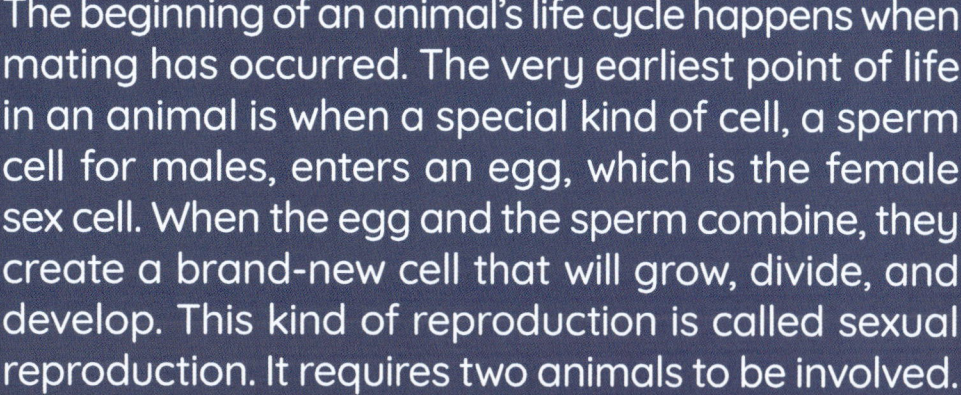

The beginning of an animal's life cycle happens when mating has occurred. The very earliest point of life in an animal is when a special kind of cell, a sperm cell for males, enters an egg, which is the female sex cell. When the egg and the sperm combine, they create a brand-new cell that will grow, divide, and develop. This kind of reproduction is called sexual reproduction. It requires two animals to be involved.

A sperm cell entering an egg. Once they combine, it will create a new cell that will grow and develop.

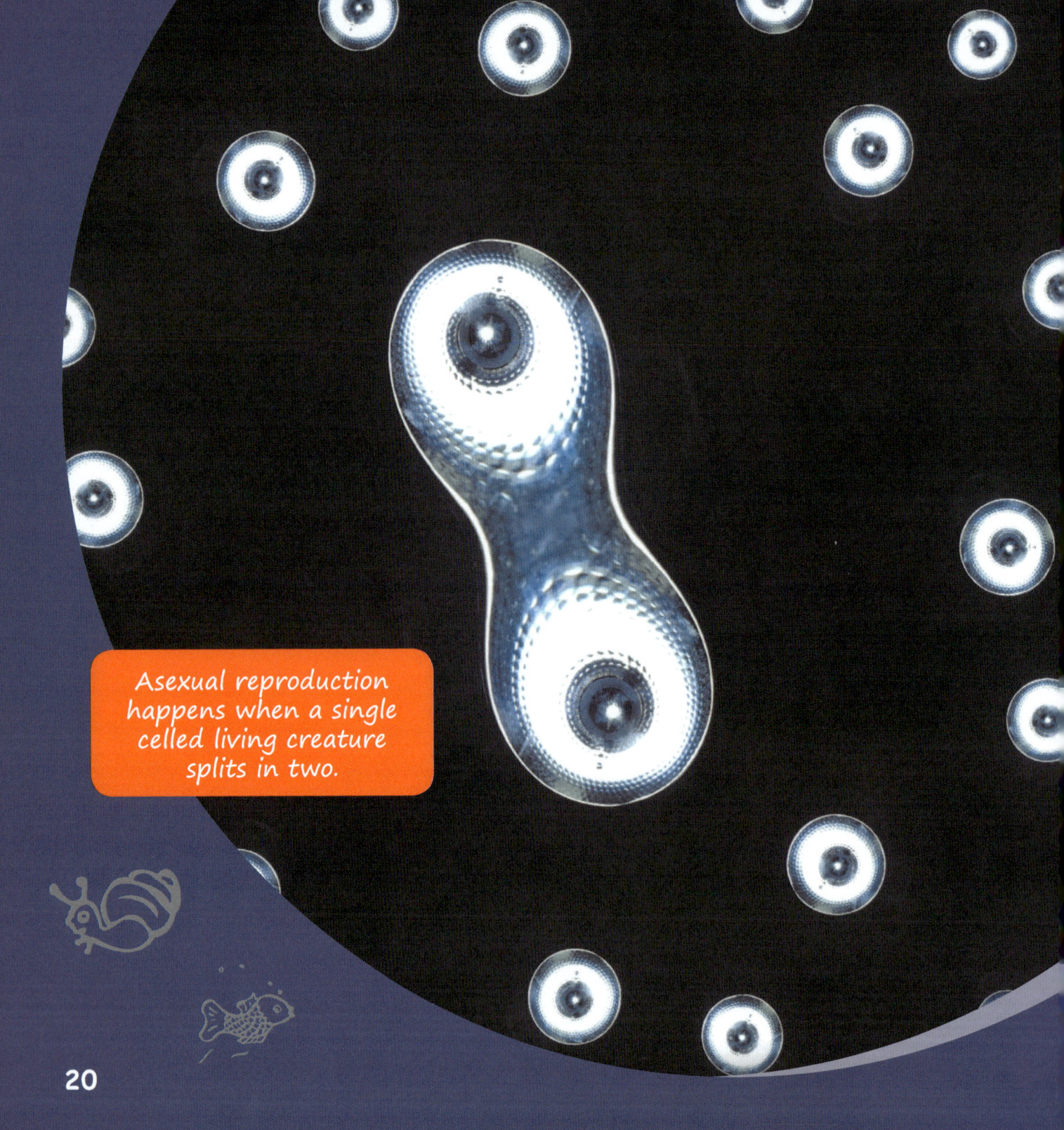

Asexual reproduction happens when a single celled living creature splits in two.

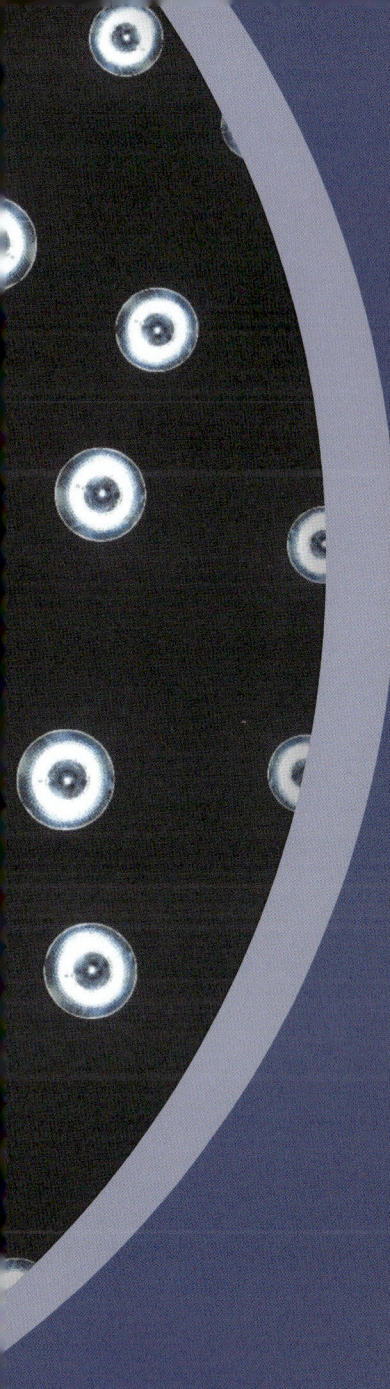

A different form of reproduction is called asexual reproduction. It happens in a process called binary fission. Fission means that something is split. Binary means two. It is a very literal description as asexual reproduction happens often when a single celled living creature, such as bacteria, splits in two. This creates two identical cells.

Unlike asexual reproduction, sexual reproduction mixes up the genes from two different sources. As a result, the offspring of sexual reproduction will not look completely the same as their parent.

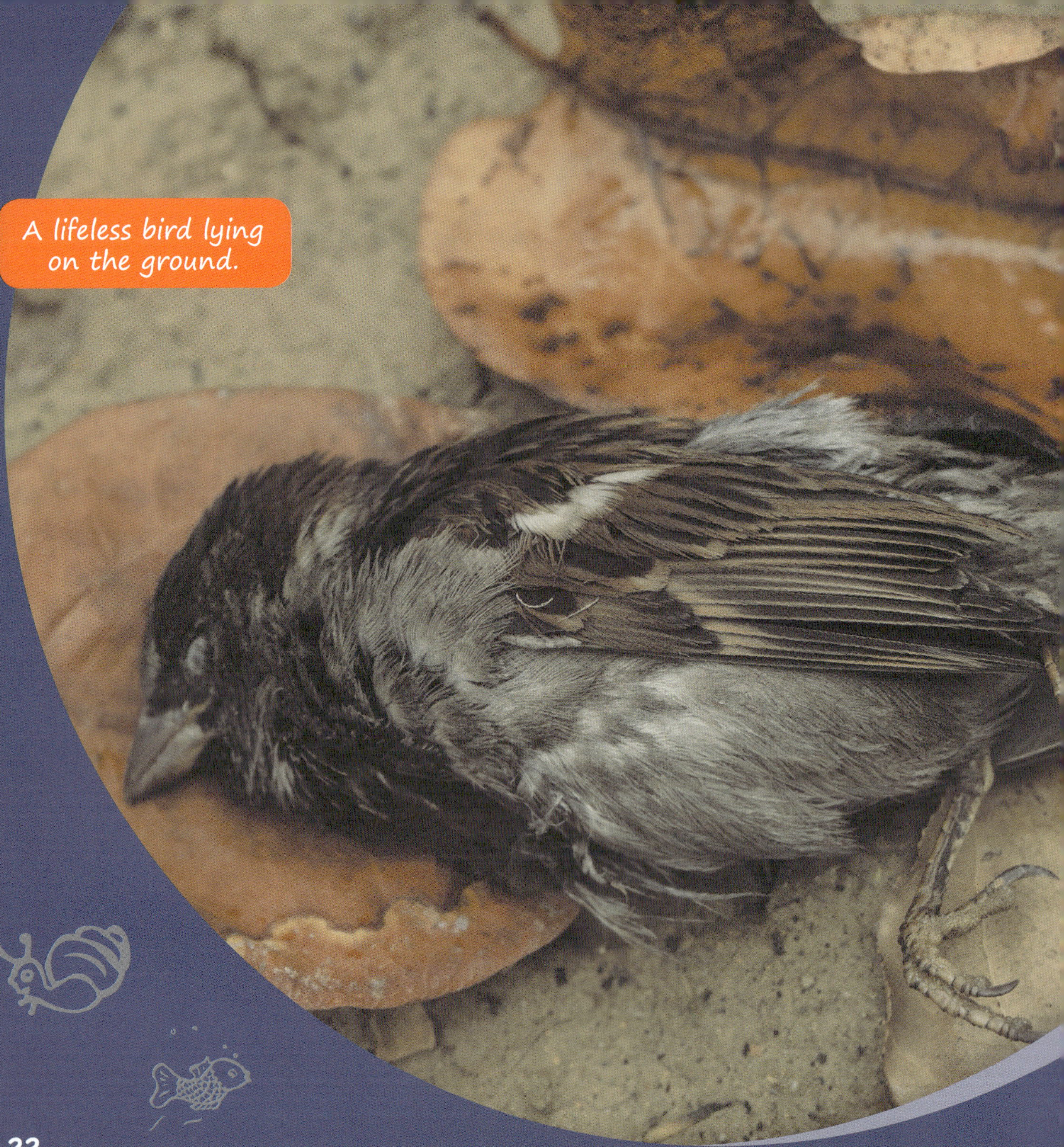

A lifeless bird lying on the ground.

Death:

The final stage of the life cycle is death. The life of every living creature will end in death. However, the length that a life lasts depends on many factors. Each species has an average life span; of course this can depend on where the animal is living as well. If it has plenty of food, water, and shelter it may live longer than if it did not have everything it needed to live well.

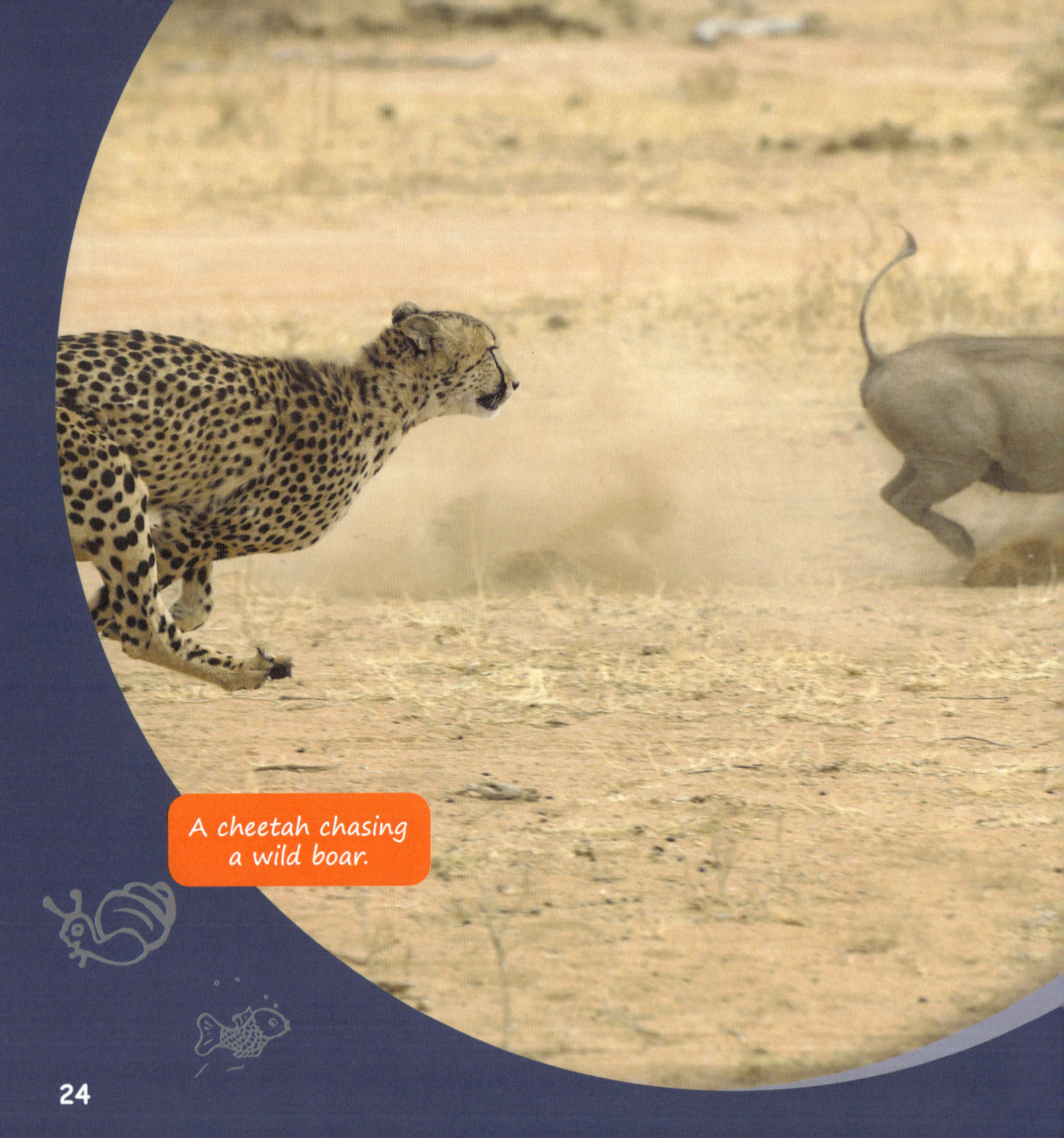

A cheetah chasing a wild boar.

It can also depend on if the animal born is healthy or not. An animal that cannot run to escape predators is not likely to live for long. Some species will have a short average lifespan compared to humans; others will have longer.

THE LIFE CYCLE OF PLANTS

A close up look of sword fern spores.

Compared to the life cycle of animals, plants are unique. They may reproduce asexually or sexually. The life cycle may begin with a spore which can reproduce all by itself. Otherwise, a plant may reproduce sexually. This would start a new life cycle. However, even though new plant life may come from sexual reproduction, this reproduction can happen all within the same plant. That is to say that a plant can reproduce with itself, even if it happens sexually.

All plants will begin as a tiny seed.

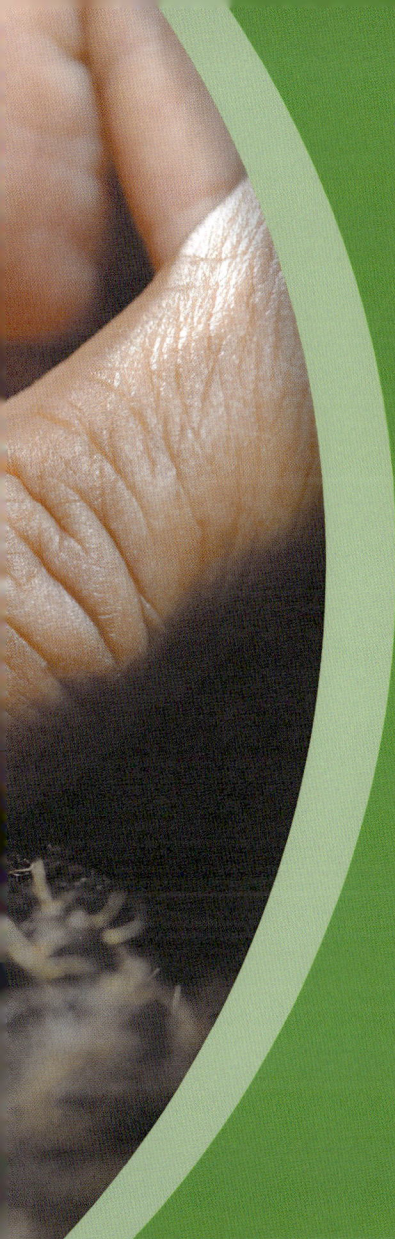

Germination:

All plants will begin as a tiny seed. It does not matter how big they grow to be. The seeds may vary in shape and size, however. A seed will contain a tiny, undeveloped plant inside of a hard, outer shell. This shell is called a seed coat and is meant to protect the seed from harm. These seeds often are formed within flowers.

An apple fruit may be eaten by wild animals and its seed dropped somewhere.

Seeds may be dropped next to their parent plant or they may be spread around by wind, water, and animals. Seeds that are in fruit, for instance, may be eaten by animals who will carry it somewhere far away. If the seed is lucky, it will find a good place to grow where it is brought. This is where the process called germination occurs.

A seed must have soil, water, and sunshine to grow. If these requirements are met, the seed will start to germinate which begins the process of growing into a brand-new plant.

A seed must have soil, water, and sunshine to grow.

A seedling starting to grow.

When the little undeveloped plant in the seed grows enough to burst out of the outer layer and poke its way out of the soil into the open air, it is called a seedling. This seedling will typically not have more than a few leaves. These leaves will capture the energy of the sun to make food and stretch roots out to gain water and nutrients from the soil. At this stage, the seedling often does not resemble the plant into which it will grow. Flowers or fruit will not develop until later.

As time passes, a seedling will mature into a young adult plant.

As time passes, a seedling will mature into a young adult plant. These plants will be thicker, stronger, and taller than they were as a seedling. Generally, they will have many more leaves and deeper and longer roots. These plants look much more like their fully mature counterparts. However, they will not yet be able to create their own flowers, fruit, or seeds.

Adulthood:

A fully mature plant is an adult plant. It can produce its own seeds and reproduce. What these seeds look like and how they are distributed will change from plant to plant. A dandelion's seeds will blow away in the wind. A pine tree will have seeds in pinecones. Some will produce seeds inside of their fruit and flowers.

Dandelion spores blown away by the wind.

A close up look of pollen in a flower.

Reproduction:

For plants that reproduce sexually, a single plant will have male and female parts. The male parts produce pollen at the stamen. This pollen can add onto the female part called the pistil. This eventually leads to the pollen fertilizing the plant's egg cells. This process is commonly thought of as happening inside a flower.

A fern is an example of a non-flowering plant.

Non-flowering plants can produce sexually or asexually. Some plants will produce spores that are small and look like they are made of dust. The spores will fly in the wind to new locations to grow. They often do best in darker, moist places.

Fern spores

Pine trees produce cones which contain seeds.

46

When sexual reproduction occurs for plants without flowers, the male and female parts are more unique. Pine or fir trees produce cones which contain seeds. Nevertheless, not all cones are the same. Some will produce the pollen; others will be fertilized to produce the seeds.

Pine cones

THE LIFE CYCLE
OF INSECTS

Insects are one of the most populous of living creatures. It is speculated that around three quarters of all animals are insects. As of today, scientists have identified around a million types of insects. New species are still being discovered. The majority of these insects will be hatched from eggs. However, it is possible for some to have live births.

An example of an insect is a dragonfly.

Insects like grasshoppers shed their skin with a new exoskeleton.

Molting:

While insects come into the world like other animals we have discussed, their growth is quite different. Insects have a hard exoskeleton. "Exo" means outside. Our skeletons, the hard parts of our body, are inside. We would call that an endoskeleton. Since insects have exoskeletons, when they grow, the exoskeleton must be shed, and a new exoskeleton must be grown. The process of shedding the old covering and growing a new one is called molting.

A butterfly undergoing metamorphosis. Starting from a caterpillar, to a pupa, and finally to an adult butterfly.

Metamorphosis:

Other insects have found a different way of growing into maturity. They go through a process called metamorphosis which changes their appearance significantly. Metamorphosis is what occurs when a caterpillar turns into a butterfly while in a cocoon.

This life cycle begins with larva. Larva typically looks more like a worm than what you would expect of an insect. It will eat large amounts and may molt several times. However, as it grows, it will reach a stage where it rests in a pupa. While it is in the pupa, it will use its energy to develop into its adult body. This will include wings and legs. Bees and moths are examples of other insects that go through this process.

Caterpillars are the larvae of butterflies and moths.

THE LIFE CYCLE OF AMPHIBIANS

An example of an amphibian is a frog.

An amphibian is what we call a creature that can live on both land and under water. Most amphibians will lay eggs. Furthermore, these eggs will typically be laid in water. Most amphibians will have a life cycle that can be largely divided into two parts.

Frogs begin their lives as tadpoles.

Larva:

Most amphibians will begin their development in the water. These kinds of larva will have a set of gills which will allow them to breathe underwater. Fish also have gills. Depending on the species of amphibian, it may remain in this stage for weeks or even years. Frogs, for example, begin their lives as tadpoles which look nothing like frogs. Tadpoles swim around in the water by wiggling their tales.

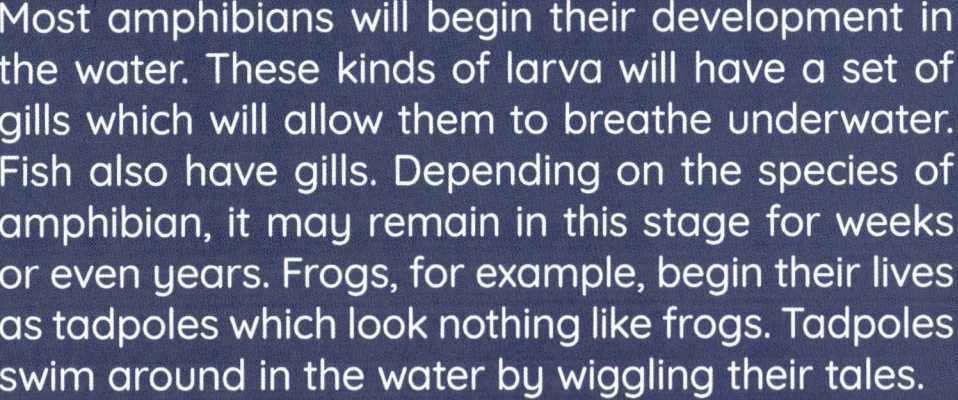

Becoming an Adult:

It is possible for some species to have larva that are the same as their adult forms, but smaller. If this is not the case, when the amphibian is ready to leave the larva form, it will often lose its gills and develop a set of lungs. This allows it to live on land for some of the time. This is also called metamorphosis as the body structure undergoes many structural changes. Tadpoles, for example, will not only develop lungs, they will lose their tails and grow legs.

A crested newt larva showing its gills.

Life cycles can look different for various species.

Life cycles describe the process of how a living organism grows up, matures, and can continue the cycle through reproduction. Life cycles can look different for various species. Some will go through metamorphosis; others will not.

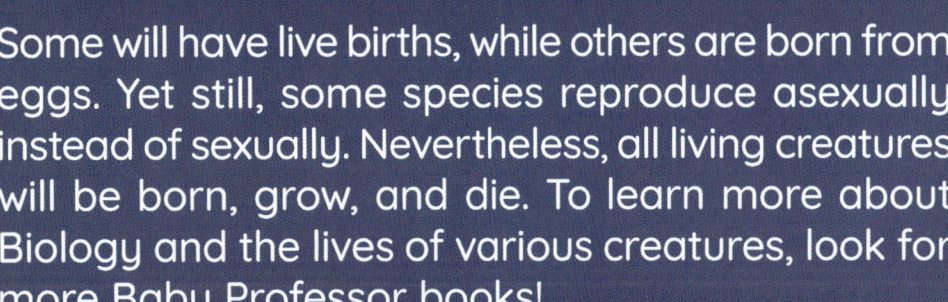

Some will have live births, while others are born from eggs. Yet still, some species reproduce asexually instead of sexually. Nevertheless, all living creatures will be born, grow, and die. To learn more about Biology and the lives of various creatures, look for more Baby Professor books!

Fish are born from eggs.

VISIT

www.speedypublishing.com

To view and download free content
on your favorite subject and browse
our catalog of new and exciting
books for readers of all ages.

Printed in Great Britain
by Amazon